My little cat

My little cat

is in the box.

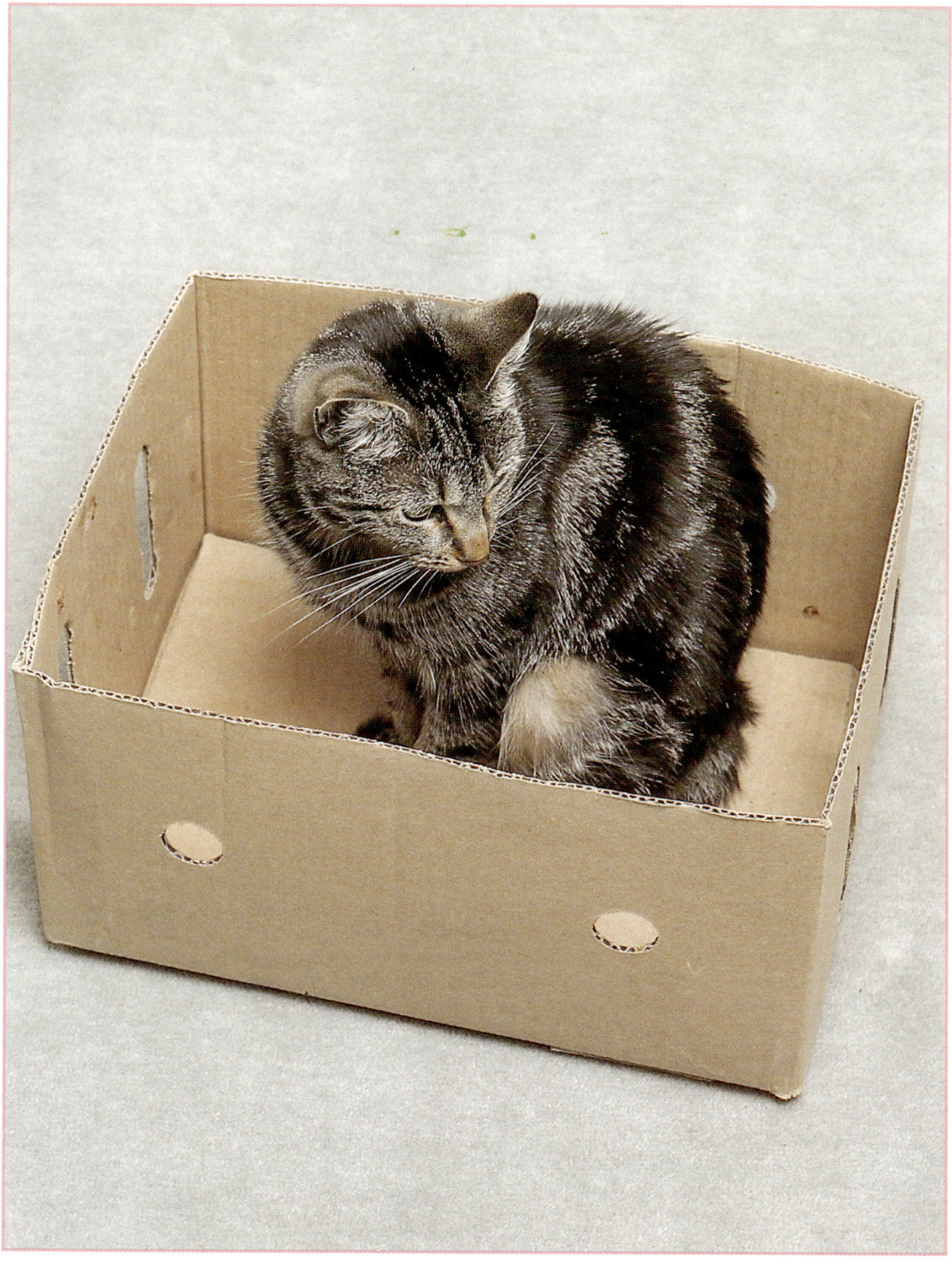

My little cat

is in the basket.

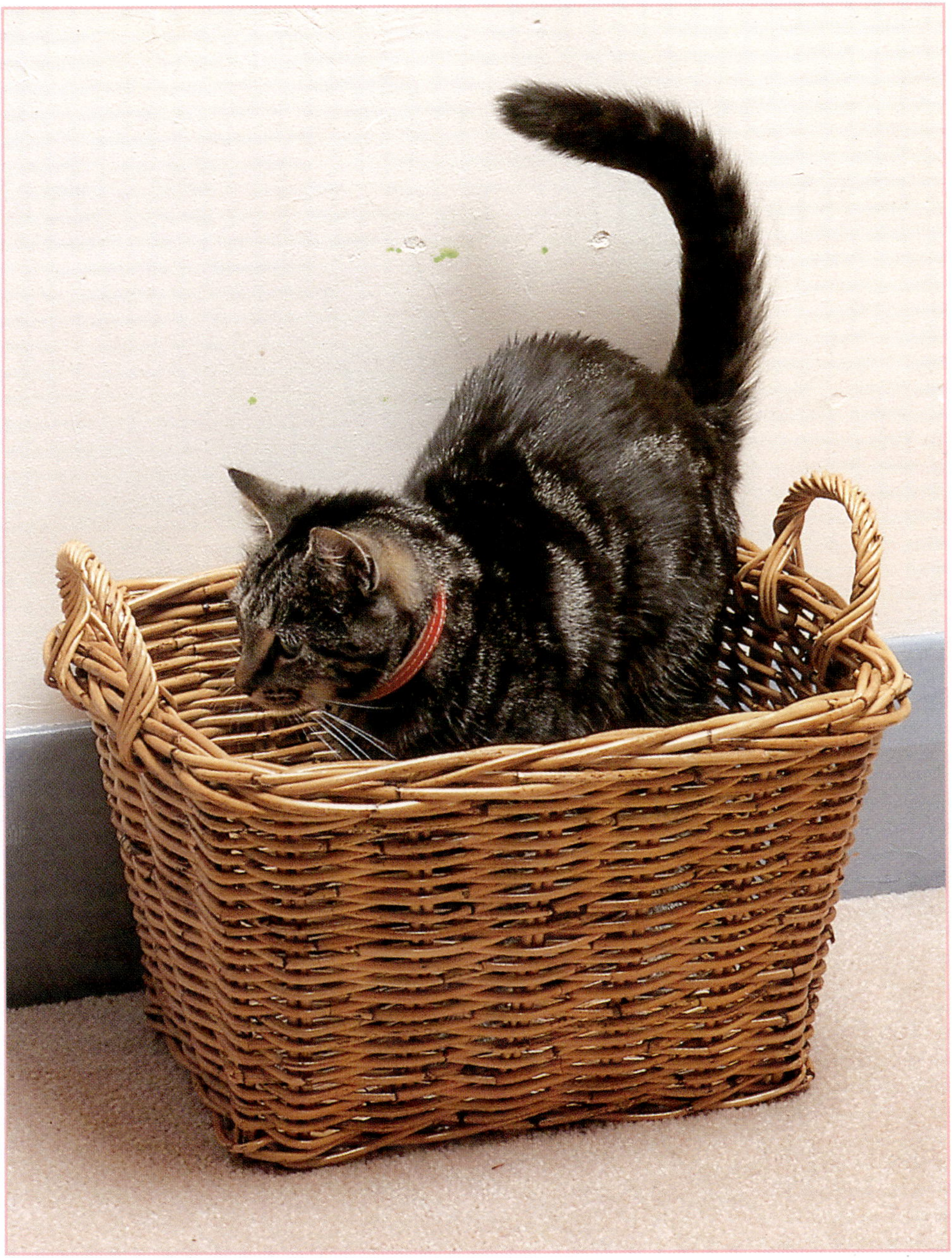

My little cat

is in the bag.

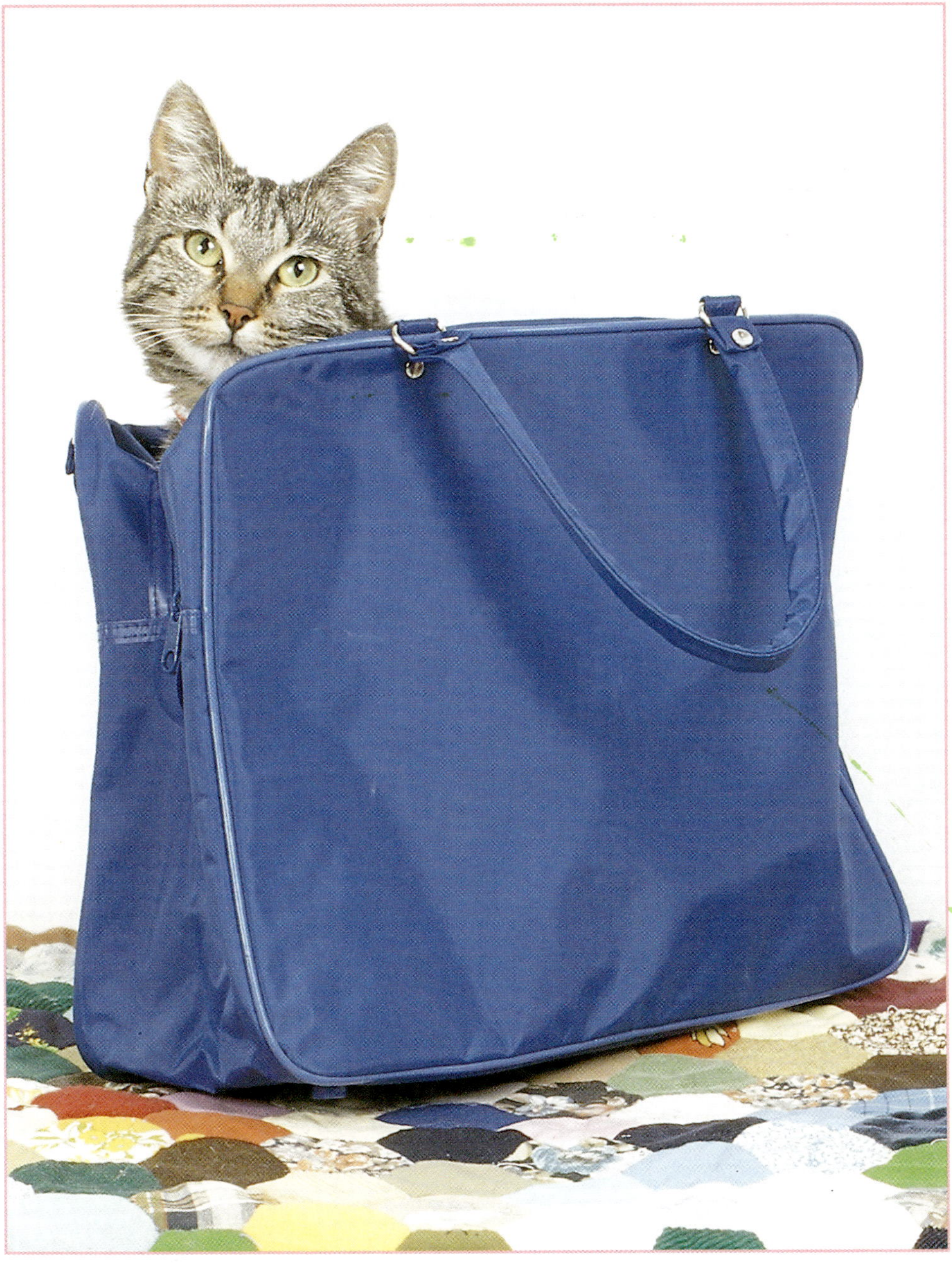

My little cat

is in the cupboard.

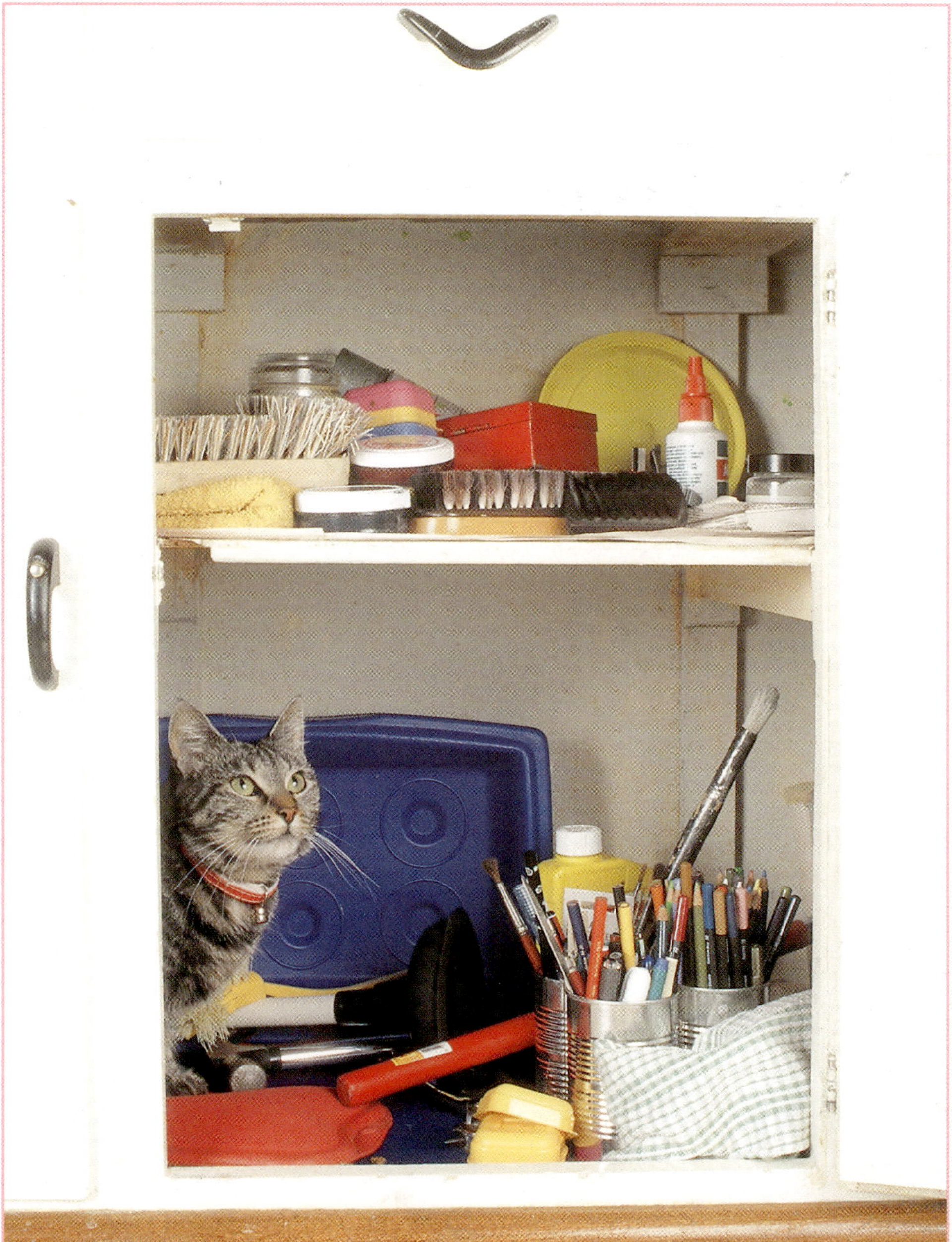

My little cat

is in the drawer.

11

My little cat

is in the bucket.

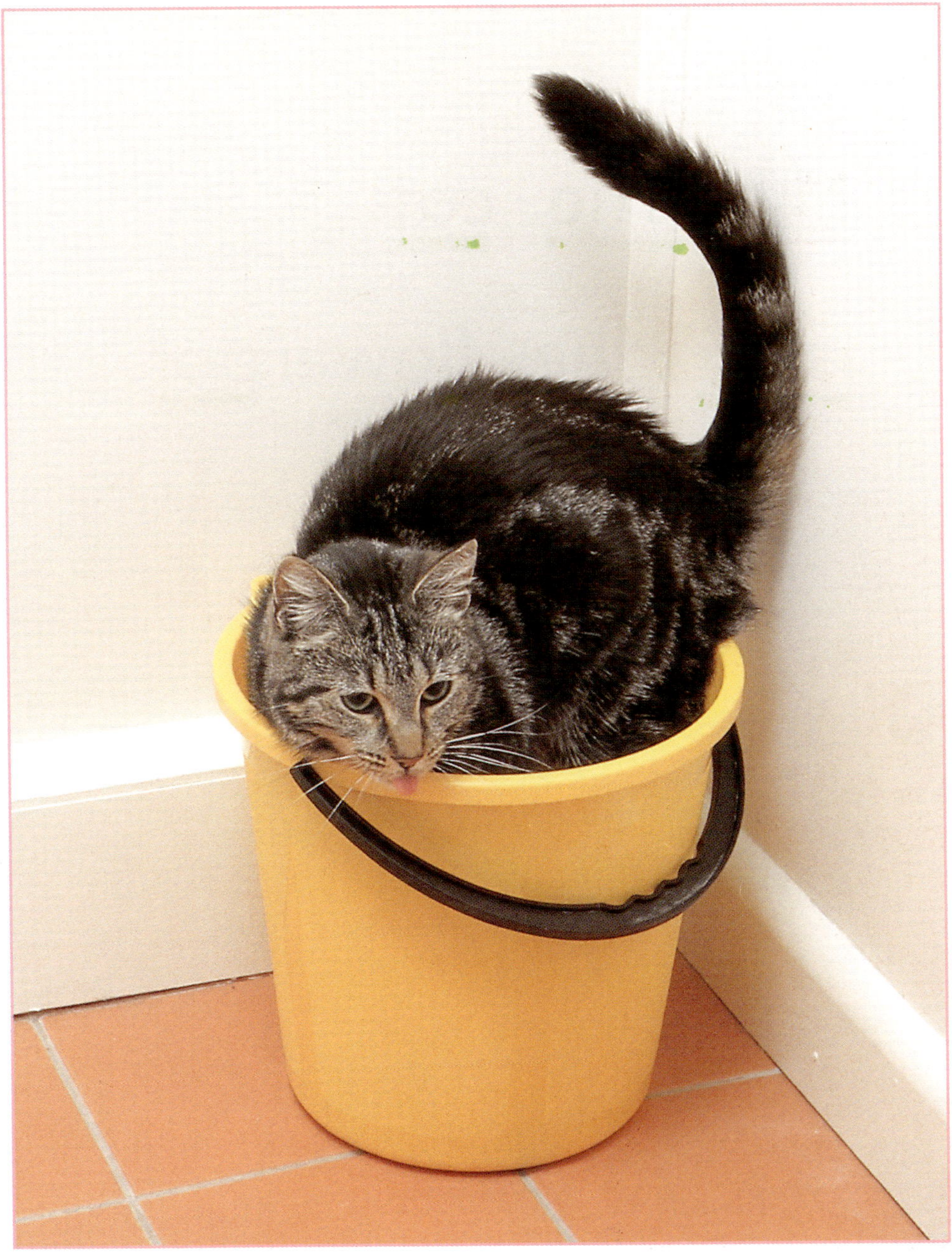

My little cat

is in the flowerpot.

My little cat
is up in the tree.